VOCAL SELECTIONS

Music by **ANDREW LLOYD WEBBER**
Lyrics by **JIM STEINMAN**

The musical works contained in this edition may not be publicly
performed in a dramatic form or context except under licence from
The Really Useful Group Limited, 22 Tower Street, London WC2H 9NS.

Exclusive Distributors:
Music Sales Limited, 8/9 Frith Street, London W1V 5TZ, England.
Music Sales Pty Limited, 120 Rothschild Avenue, Rosebery, NSW 2018, Australia.
www.musicinprint.com

This book © Copyright 1998 by The Really Useful Group Limited.
Order No. RG10369
ISBN 0-7119-7295-8

Production photographs by Ivan Kyncl. Studio photographs by Sasha Gusov.
Music preparation by Dakota Music Services. Music arranged by David Cullen.
Cover artwork by Dewynters Limited, London.

World première at the Aldwych Theatre, 1 July 1998.

Music Sales' complete catalogue describes thousands of titles and is
available in full colour sections by subject, direct from Music Sales Limited.
Please state your areas of interest and send a cheque/postal order for £1.50 for postage to:
Music Sales Limited, Newmarket Road, Bury St. Edmunds, Suffolk IP33 3YB.

Printed in the United Kingdom by Halstan & Co Limited, Amersham, Buckinghamshire.

THE VAULTS OF HEAVEN

Music by **ANDREW LLOYD WEBBER**. Lyrics by **JIM STEINMAN**.

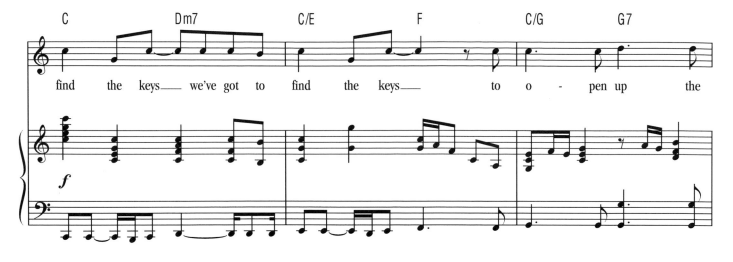

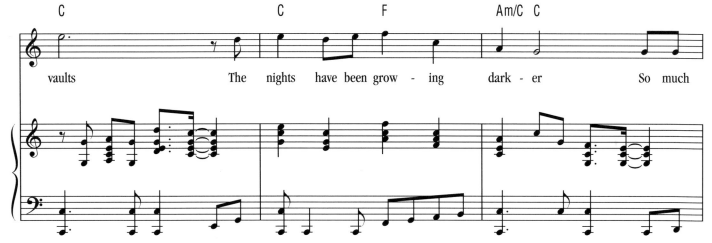

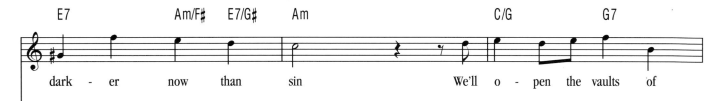

WHISTLE DOWN THE WIND

Music by **ANDREW LLOYD WEBBER**. Lyrics by **JIM STEINMAN**.

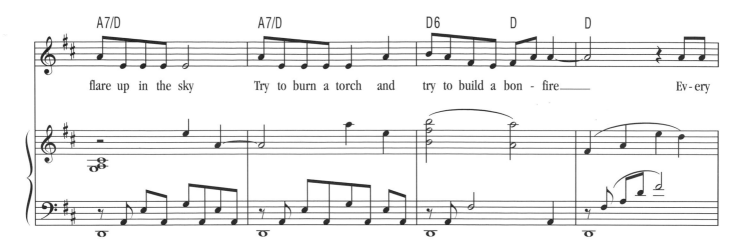

flare up in the sky   Try to burn a torch and   try to build a bon - fire___   Ev - ery

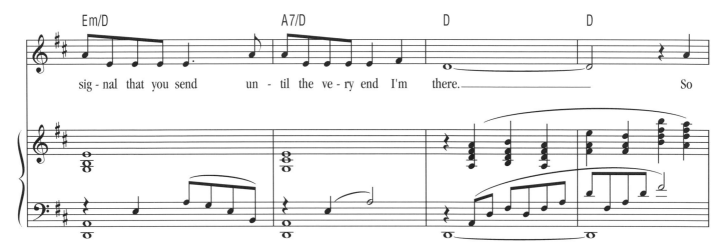

sig - nal that you send   un - til the ve - ry end I'm   there.___   So

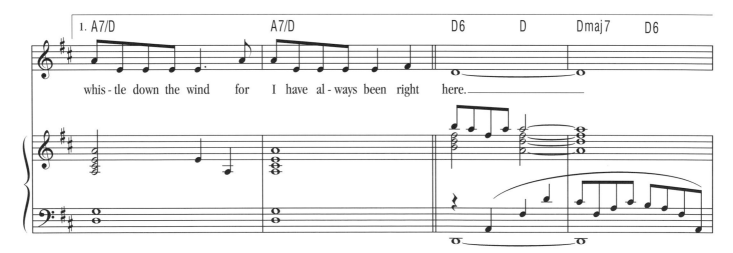

1. whis - tle down the wind   for   I have al - ways been right   here.___

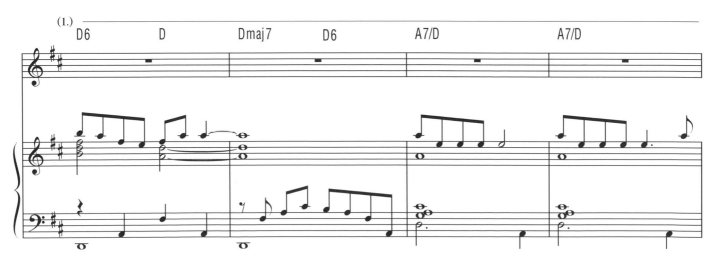

(1.)

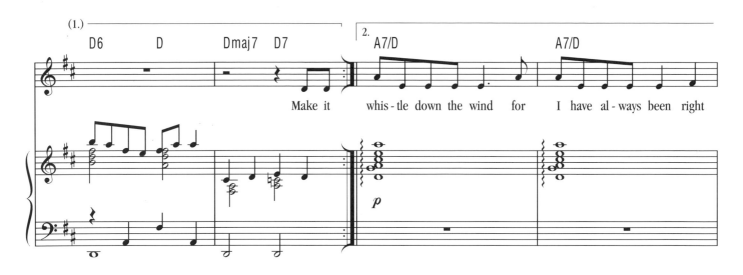

Make it whis-tle down the wind for I have al-ways been right

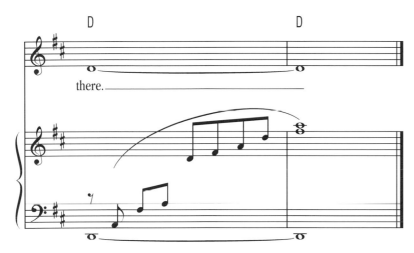

there.

COLD

Music by **ANDREW LLOYD WEBBER**. Lyrics by **JIM STEINMAN**.

Medium Blues Rock

Edward

1. The flow-ers have all died the skies are go-ing grey I
got-ta see my girl I got-ta see her eyes the bar-

begged my ba-by not to leave I could-n't make her stay the heat has dis-ap-peared the et-
o-me-ter is fall-ing on-ly she can make it rise there's no-thing on the trees there's

er - nal flame is low the fore - cast ain't so good I'm all messed up no place to go.
no - thing for me here I'm search - ing for sal - va - tion and some ther - mal un - der - wear it's

Cold like a froz - en tear drop
cold and it's get - ting cold - er

there's a chill in the air and there's ice in my veins and it won't
they're e - va - cu - a - ting Sa - tan who's wait ing for hell to freeze ov -

stop Cold
er Lord it's cold

it's an end - less win - ter___ the

moon's on the run___ and ev - en the sun___ is cold___

1.

2. I

2. The moon's on the run___ and ev - en the sun___ is cold___

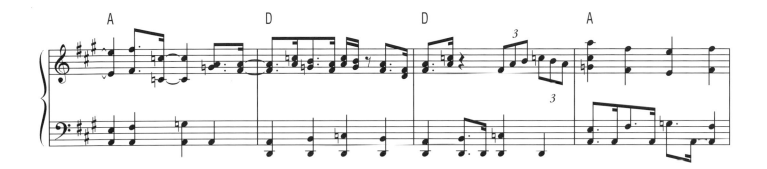

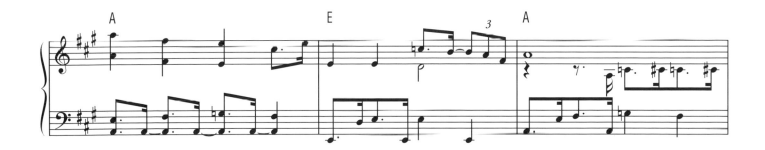

I gotta see my girl I gotta see her eyes the bar-
ometer is falling only she can make it rise there's nothing on the trees there's
nothing for me here I gotta find salvation and some thermal underwear It's
cold_____ and it's getting colder_____

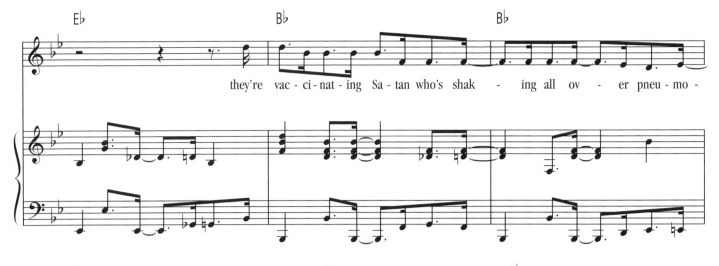

they're vac - ci - nat - ing Sa - tan who's shak - - ing all ov - - er pneu - mo -

nia___ Cold___

_ like an end - less win - ter___ the

moon's on the run___ and ev - en the sun___ is cold___

The stars are all gone_____ and ev-en the sun_____ is cold_____

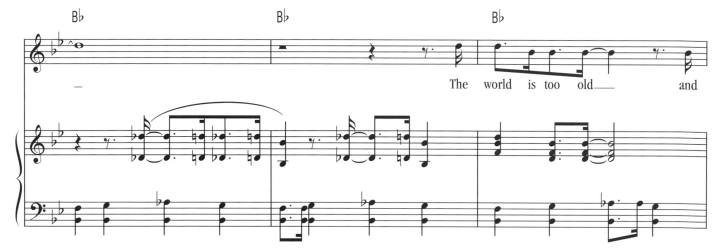

The world is too old_____ and

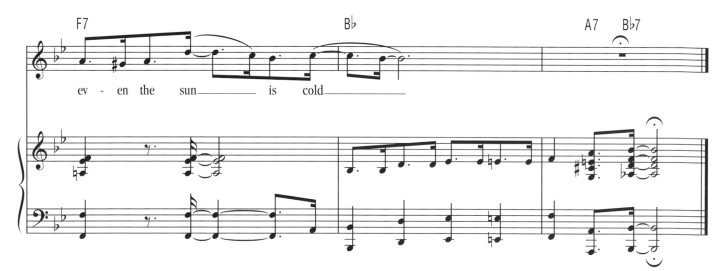

ev - en the sun_____ is cold_____

UNSETTLED SCORES

Music by **ANDREW LLOYD WEBBER**. Lyrics by **JIM STEINMAN**.

Moderato (Rubato)

Man
There's a prayer for the liv-ing and the dy-ing, There's a prayer to soothe the sav-age sea. There's a

prayer it seems for al-most ev-'ry thing But___ you have-n't got a prayer for

Rit.

Più Mosso

me. And___ I I have-n't got a prayer. So man-y

mf

mf

cries in the night that you try to ig-nore Why did-n't I do that?___ Why did-n't I do this?___

mp

___ So ma-ny un-brok-en chains so man-y un-set-tled scores.___ The

her - oes on the play - ing field for - got - ten in a day. The

priest in the con-fes-sion-al, the trem-bling hands and whis-pered sighs, the doc-tors at the hos-pit-al un -

end - ing tests and twist - ed lies. The be - tray - ers, the be - trayed, the ab -

an - doned, the a - fraid, The cor - rup-ted and the cel - e - brat-ed, end-less - ly hum - il - i - a - ted

cresc

(cresc)

glo - ri - ous - ly big par - ade. You can say a prayer for ev - 'ry - one___ that there could ev - er

be, say a prayer for all of these and more___ but there's still no prayer for me. Say a

prayer for your pur - est daugh - ter, Toll a bell for your on - ly son. There's

no way out and all my prayers are fad - ing one by one. The

stern and dis - ap - prov - ing lips, The friends who just at - tack. The

fath - ers that they take a - way, The ones that can't get back. The

des - p'rate boy who sleeps a - lone who - ev - er's in his bed. The

chos - en ones they get a home, the bles - sed get a - head. The

kids out play - ing soft - ball in the fa - ding sum - mer night, The teen - age lov - ers at the drive - in The glow of the dash - board light. An Am - er - i - can Fly - er on a steep in - cline, The wind blow - ing through your hair The tro - phies and the hol - i - days they van - ished in the air, The be -

trayers, the be-trayed, The ab-an-doned, the a-fraid, the glo-ri-fied the i-do-lized, The

bas-tards and their jea-lous eyes. An am- az-ing-ly big par-ade! You can

say a prayer for ev-'ry-one___ you've known or you might see, Say a

prayer for all of these and more___ but there's still no prayer for me. Say a

prayer for ev - 'ry liv - ing thing, the un - born and de - ceased, But I have - n't got a

prayer I know, That's the na - ture of the beast.

That's the

na - ture of the beast.

IF ONLY

Music by **ANDREW LLOYD WEBBER**. Lyrics by **JIM STEINMAN**.

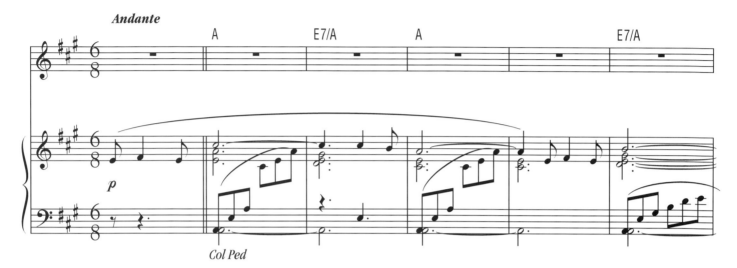

on — ly it was so — These are the lone —

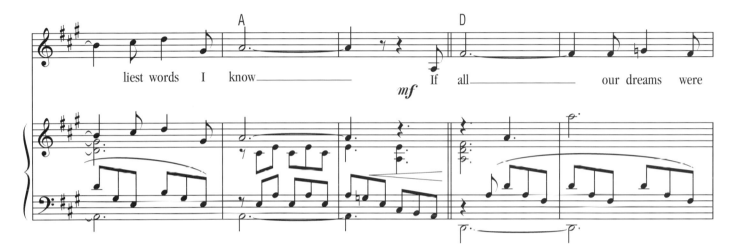

liest words I know — If all — our dreams were

mf

gold - en — and ne — ver black or grey —

If all — our dreams came true then — we'd

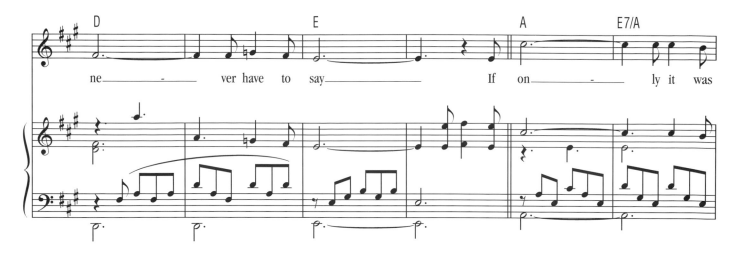

ne_____ - ____ver have to say_____ If on_____ - _____ly it was

so_____ These are the lone_____ - _____liest words I know.

Poco Rit.

Man

If all I've lost_____ some-how came back_____ If all that

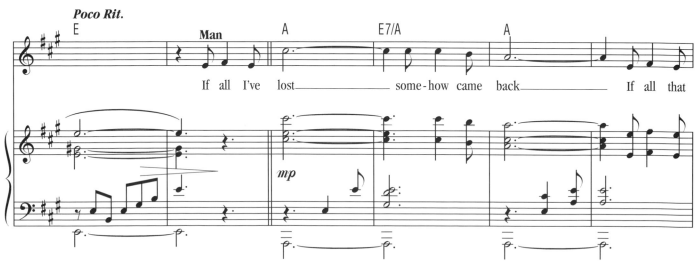

died _____ a-gain would grow _____ If on _____ ly it was

so _____ These are the lone _____ liest words I know. _____

NO MATTER WHAT

Music by **ANDREW LLOYD WEBBER**. Lyrics by **JIM STEINMAN**.

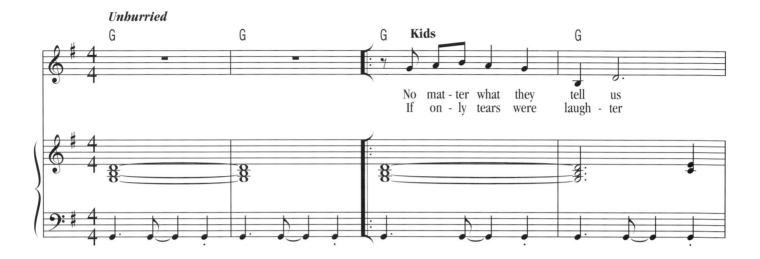

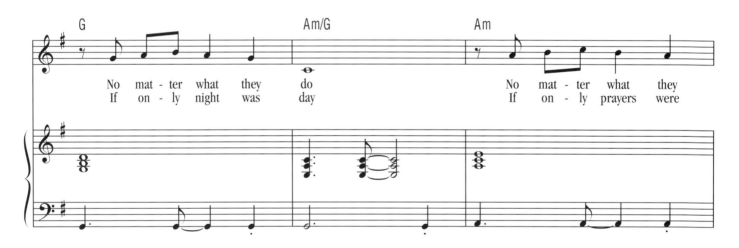

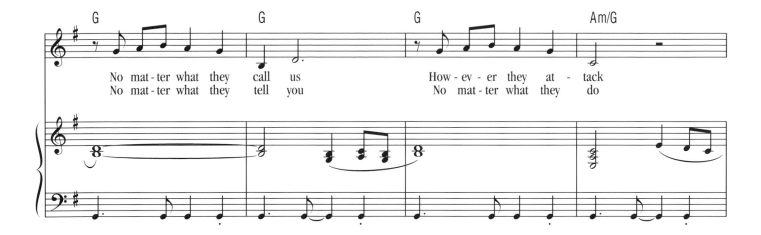

No mat-ter what they call us How-ev-er they at-tack
No mat-ter what they tell you No mat-ter what they do

No mat-ter where they take us We'll find our own way back_____ I
No mat-ter what they teach you What you be-lieve is true_____ And

can't de-ny_____ what I_____ be-lieve_____ I can't be_____ what I'm not
I will keep_____ you safe_____ and strong_____ And shelt-ered_____ from the storm

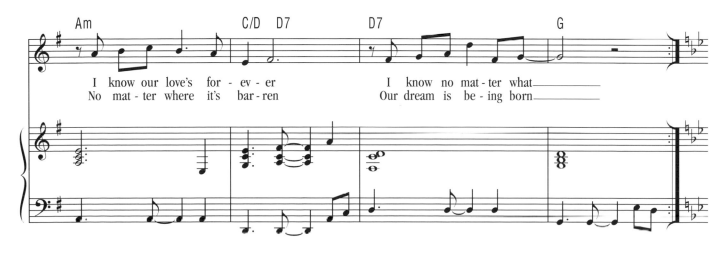

I know our love's for-ev-er I know no mat-ter what_____
No mat-ter where it's bar-ren Our dream is be-ing born_____

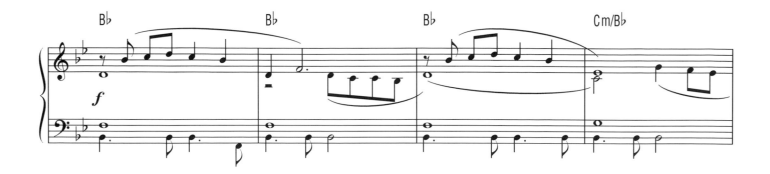

No mat-ter who they fol-low No mat-ter where they lead

No mat-ter how they judge us I'll be eve-ry-one you need No

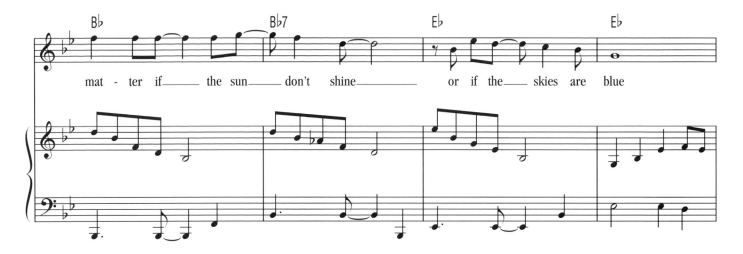

mat - ter if____ the sun____ don't shine_____ or if the____ skies are blue

No mat - ter what the end - ing my life be - gan with you I

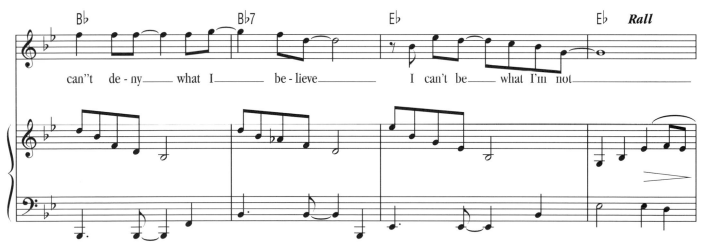

can''t de - ny____ what I____ be - lieve_____ I can't be____ what I'm not____

I know this love's for - ev - er I know no mat - ter what

37

WHEN CHILDREN RULE THE WORLD

Music by **ANDREW LLOYD WEBBER**. Lyrics by **JIM STEINMAN**.

children rule the world_____ When child-ren rule the world_____ to-night- When

child-ren rule the world._____ All the great-est wish-es are grant-ed

Let us sing let in-no-cence reign_____ All the prayers are

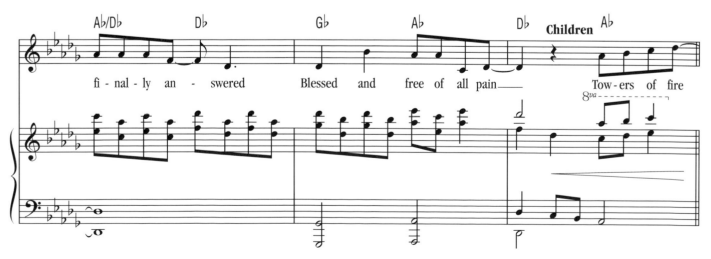

fi-nal-ly an-swered Blessed and free of all pain_____ Tow-ers of fire

rise ev - er higher_____ mag - ic - al flags_____ will be un - furled_____

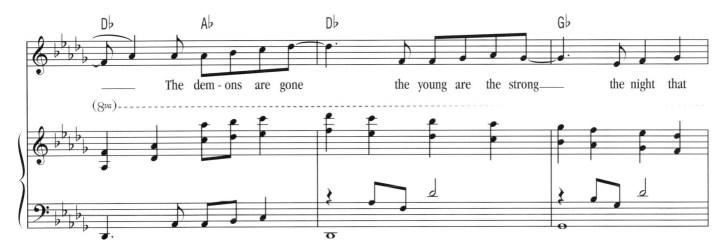

_____ The dem - ons are gone the young are the strong_____ the night that

child - ren rule the world_____ When child - ren rule the world_____ to - night_____ When

child - ren rule the world_____ Tow - ers of fire rise ev - er higher_____

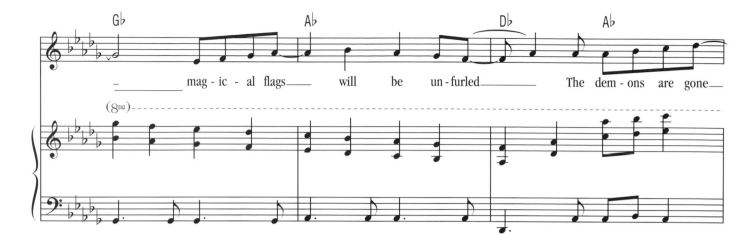

mag - ic - al flags will be un-furled The dem - ons are gone

the young are the strong the night that child - ren rule the world When

child - ren rule the world to - night When child - ren rule the world When

child - ren rule the world to - night when child - ren rule the world!

A KISS IS A TERRIBLE THING TO WASTE

Music by **ANDREW LLOYD WEBBER**. Lyrics by **JIM STEINMAN**.

Bm   G   F#sus   F#   Bm   2. + Swallow

clo - ser to me now like we're shar - ing the same skin____ We got - ta
trem - ble when we touch Let me show you what to do and how____ Cause we'll

G   D   G   D   1. Amos / 2. Man

get out of this jail, we got - ta let the fu - ture in So ma - ny
ne - ver be as young as we are____ right now.____ So ma - ny

B♭m   F   G♭ 2. Amos G♭   D♭   2. Man G♭   D♭

things in your life that you're bound to re-gret Why did-n't I do that?____ Why did-n't I do this?____
cries in the night that you try to ig-nore Why did-n't I do this?____ Why did-n't I do that?____

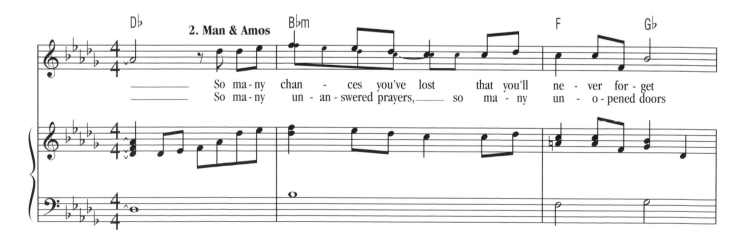

D♭   2. Man & Amos   B♭m   F   G♭

____ So ma - ny chan - ces you've lost that you'll ne - ver for-get
____ So ma - ny un - an - swered prayers,____ so ma - ny un - o - pened doors

44

Gb Db Gb Db Db **Amos & Man**

Why did-n't I make it? Why did-n't I take it right there?
Why did-n't I take it? Why did-n't I make it come true?
The

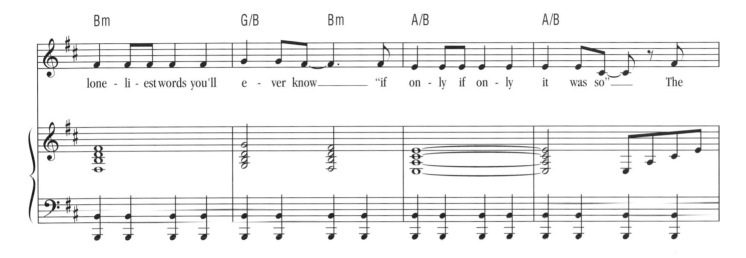

Bm G/B Bm A/B A/B

lone - li - est words you'll e - ver know___ "if on - ly if on - ly it was so"___ The

Bm G/B Bm A/B A/B

emp - ti - est words that they'll e - ver be___ "It could have been me___ It could have been me"___ The

Bm G/B Bm A/B A/B

lone - lie - est words you'll e - ver know___ "If on - ly if on - ly it were so!"___ The

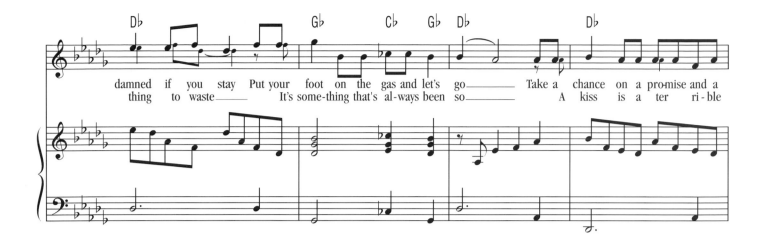

damned if you stay Put your foot on the gas and let's go_____ Take a chance on a pro-mise and a
thing to waste_____ It's some-thing that's al-ways been so_____ A kiss is a ter ri - ble

roll of the dice We can set a few fires, we can melt all the ice_____ We can
thing to waste_____ You make one mis-take and it can't be e - rased_____ And

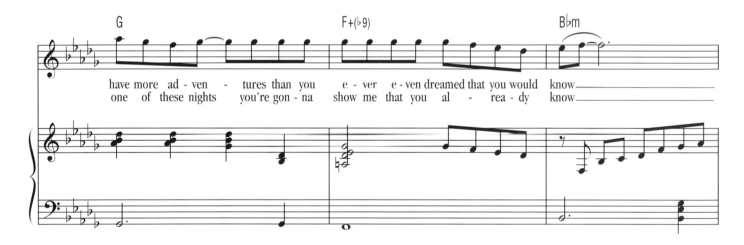

have more ad - ven - tures than you e - ver e - ven dreamed that you would know_____
one of these nights you're gon - na show me that you al - rea - dy know_____

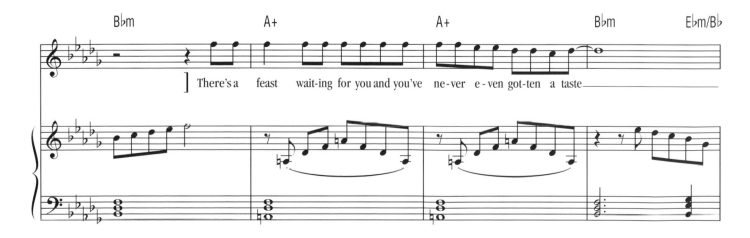

There's a feast wait-ing for you and you've ne - ver e - ven got-ten a taste_____

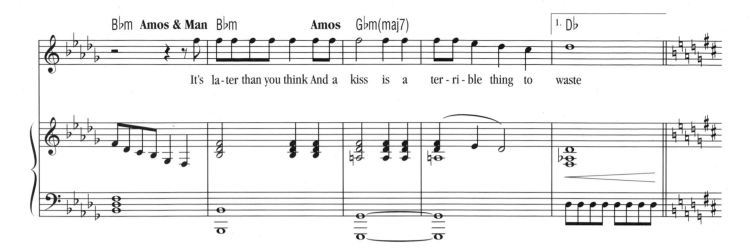

It's la-ter than you think And a kiss is a ter-ri-ble thing to waste

2. If you

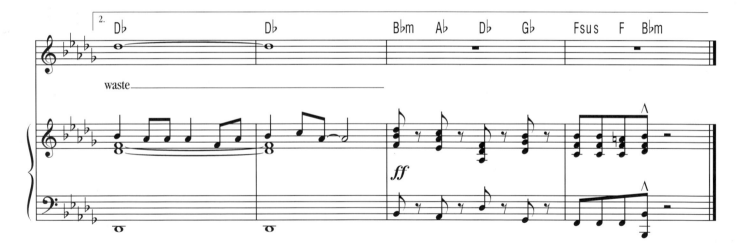

waste